TOO OLD TO ROCK AND ROLL
and Other Stories

Do you understand your parents? Do your parents understand you? It's not always easy to be a teenager – as these three stories show.

Greg plays in a rock band, is good at cooking, and tries to help his father after his mother's death. What poor old Dad needs, Greg thinks, is a nice, kind, sensible friend – like Valerie. But Greg's Dad has other plans . . .

Then we meet a girl who goes to have tea with a schoolfriend. But it's not a visit that she could ever tell her mother about . . .

And last, there's Daniel, who listens through the wall to the four students in the house next door. He never sees them, but he learns a lot about them . . .

OXFORD BOOKWORMS LIBRARY
Human Interest

Too Old to Rock and Roll
and Other Stories
Stage 2 (700 headwords)

Series Editor: Jennifer Bassett
Founder Editor: Tricia Hedge
Activities Editors: Jennifer Bassett and Alison Baxter

JAN MARK

Too Old to Rock and Roll

and Other Stories

Retold by
Diane Mowat

OXFORD UNIVERSITY PRESS

Oxford University Press
Great Clarendon Street, Oxford OX2 6DP

Oxford New York

Athens Auckland Bangkok Bogotá Buenos Aires Cape Town
Chennai Dar es Salaam Delhi Florence Hong Kong Istanbul Karachi Kolkata
Kuala Lumpur Madrid Melbourne Mexico City Mumbai Nairobi
Paris São Paulo Shanghai Singapore Taipei Tokyo Toronto Warsaw
with associated companies in
Berlin Ibadan

OXFORD and OXFORD ENGLISH
are trade marks of Oxford University Press

ISBN 0 19 422988 2

Original edition © Jan Mark 1990
First published by The Bodley Head 1990
This simplified edition © Oxford University Press 2000

Third impression 2001

First published in Oxford Bookworms 1994
This second edition published in the Oxford Bookworms Library 2000

Illustrated by Elizabeth Sawyer

The story 'Invitation to Tea' was originally published as 'Front'
in the volume *A Can of Worms and other stories* by Jan Mark.

Typeset by Wyvern Typesetting Ltd, Bristol
Printed in Spain by Unigraf s.l.

CONTENTS

TOO OLD TO ROCK AND ROLL

'Why don't you both stop it?' Valerie's voice said on the phone.

'Well, Dad began it,' Greg answered. 'He called me a baby.'

'And you called him an old man. That wasn't nice.'

'I didn't really mean it. He isn't very old, is he?' Greg said. He remembered that Valerie was about forty herself.

'No. And what about that piece from the newspaper about older men losing their hair? You put that up on the kitchen wall! You've got to stop it,' Valerie said.

'Why don't you both stop it?' Valerie's voice said on the phone.

'We need someone here to stop us,' Greg said quietly.

'I know,' Valerie spoke softly now. 'Well, I'll be there at eight o'clock tonight. I'll see you then, all right?'

Greg put the phone down and went into the kitchen. He looked at the piece from the newspaper about men losing their hair. Near it on the wall there was a piece of paper with Mum's writing on it. Perhaps it was the only thing of Mum's in the house now. Dad took away all her things when she died.

Dad still had a lot of hair. It was only a bit thin on the top of his head. And he did it differently now. It showed that he was getting better after Mum's death. At first he didn't want to do anything. Greg watched him in those first weeks. Dad got up, read the newspaper, cooked meals, went to work – but he was dead inside. When he was at work, Dad was Stephen Barber the optician. Perhaps there he smiled and talked and was more like a living person. But he wasn't like that at home.

Things were getting better now because of Valerie. She was a friend of Mum's really, and was waiting to see Mum when the unhappy policeman came to the house to tell them about the accident. She lived about fifty kilometres away and had a home to go back to. But the policeman wanted to take Dad and Greg to the hospital and Dad turned to this stranger and said, 'Please stay.' So when they came back, she was there.

And Christmas happened because of Valerie, too. Greg said nothing about Christmas, but one day Valerie said angrily to Dad, 'And what about Greg, Steve?'

'He isn't interested in Christmas,' Dad answered tiredly. 'Christmas was wonderful with Frances. Without her, it's nothing.'

'Well, Frances is dead, but you and Greg are alive. If Christmas with Frances was wonderful, it was because she loved it. Can't you keep alive something she loved? Can't you do it for her?'

Later Greg said to Valerie, 'Are you coming here for Christmas?'

'I usually visit my mother and father,' she replied.

But Greg knew that Valerie must come. 'If Christmas doesn't happen this year,' he thought, 'perhaps it will never happen again.'

'Tell me about Christmas with your Mum, Greg,' Valerie said.

And Greg told her how he and his mother always put the decorations on the Christmas tree together.

'I've got all the things for the tree in my room,' he said. 'I hid them there when Dad took everything of Mum's away.'

'Well, we've got to be hard with him,' Valerie said. 'If we want to bring him back to life, we'll have to be a bit unkind to him. Wake him up a little.'

And so, on Christmas Eve, just before Valerie arrived,

*Greg and his mother always put the decorations
on the Christmas tree together.*

Greg came downstairs with the box of decorations for the tree.

His father looked old and tired. 'What have you got there?' he said.

'The decorations for the tree,' Greg answered.

'What tree? We aren't having a tree. How could you—'

'What have you got there?' Greg's father said.

'*I* want a tree,' Greg said. 'I'm sure that Mum wants Christmas to be happy for me.'

His father looked round slowly. 'It's too late to get a tree now,' he said.

'Valerie's bringing it with her,' Greg replied. 'Shall I light the fire?'

* * *

After Christmas life was easier. Valerie came more often and she stayed for the weekend. They began to call the third bedroom 'Valerie's room'.

Slowly, Dad was beginning to come back to life. He bought some new clothes too, and Greg was pleased about that. But perhaps the piece about older men losing their hair was unkind, Greg thought. He took the piece of newspaper off the kitchen wall, and wrote a note in its place.

I'VE GONE TO BAND PRACTICE. VAL PHONED. SHE'LL BE HERE AT EIGHT.

Then he put the dinner to cook slowly while he was out. The table was ready, with flowers on it, and everything looked just right. Greg usually cooked the meals. He was good at it, and he liked everything to be nice for his Dad and Val.

The band practice was at a friend's house, and Greg began to go there five months after Mum's death. He just wanted to get out of the house sometimes, but he told Dad he was interested in music.

The band practice was at a friend's house.

'Music?' Dad said, 'or Rock and Roll?'

'Rock and Roll was in the 1950s,' Greg told him. 'It's rock music these days.'

After the practice that evening, Greg wanted to get home

quickly. He wanted to hear happy voices and listen to the nice things that Valerie said about his cooking. So he said goodbye to his friends and hurried home.

The light was on in the living room when he arrived, and for a minute he watched from outside. Dad was standing alone in the room, with his back to the window, but Valerie's car was outside the house. Then Valerie came into the living room, and his father walked over to her with his arms open.

Greg went round to the back door very slowly. He wanted to give them more time together. He felt very pleased that his plan was going well. He liked Valerie a lot, and often told Dad that he liked her. There was no hurry, but if one day Dad and Valerie . . . He would never forget Mum, of course. Sometimes he thought that he could see her in the house or the garden. But he knew that Valerie understood this.

When Greg went in, they were sitting down again. There were a lot of flowers in the room – red, pink, orange and yellow.

'Valerie brought them,' Dad said, smiling.

Greg remembered Valerie's beautiful walled garden with its bright flowers. It was warm there even in March. Did Valerie want to leave all that? He looked at Dad. Something was different. Dad's clothes were new and he was wearing jeans. His father was wearing *jeans*! And he was smiling.

His father was wearing jeans!

10

His father was Stephen Barber again. He was the bright and happy man who married Mum.

At dinner Dad tried hard to please Valerie. In the old days Dad didn't have to try to please women. They all loved him. The two girls who worked with him at the optician's loved him too.

Greg asked his mother about this once, but she wasn't unhappy about it. She just laughed. 'Oh, yes, they both love him,' she said.

'What about you?' Greg asked angrily.

'Oh, they think I don't understand him. I'm sure they'll be happy if I fall under a bus.'

But it wasn't a bus. She was driving her car when the accident happened. How did the two women in the optician's feel now? They were both young and beautiful. Valerie wasn't young or beautiful, but she was right, just right.

When he went up to bed that night, Greg left his door open and he could hear Dad and Valerie downstairs. They were talking and laughing together for hours.

It was very late when they came to bed.

* * *

So Dad was alive again. The next week he bought more clothes for himself and for Greg. His new clothes were much more fashionable than his old ones. And at the weekend he and Valerie went out on Saturday and Sunday. Greg watched from his bedroom window. When they were

11

getting into the car, Dad ran to open the door for Valerie. He no longer looked like a tired old man, Greg thought. In his new clothes, he looked slim and young.

On Wednesday Dad came home early and said he was going to a party. 'It's Yvonne at the shop,' he said. 'She's going to get married.'

'A party?' Greg said. 'You won't like the music, or the dancing. Yvonne's much younger than you, and you don't like my music. Is Valerie going?'

'Valerie? Of course not. I'm sure she's got better things to do.'

Greg thought back to the old days. Dad and Mum often went to quiet dinner parties with friends, but never to a party with dancing, with people who were twenty years younger. Greg didn't like it.

It was after midnight when Dad came home.

* * *

Valerie came as usual on Friday. Greg cooked the dinner and then he went into the kitchen to get some drinks ready for them. But when Valerie arrived, Dad didn't hurry down to open the door as usual and Greg had to go himself. He took Valerie's bags from her and they went into the front room. Just then Greg heard Dad put the phone down in the bedroom upstairs.

After a while Dad came downstairs and went into the front room. Greg gave him some time alone with Valerie

12

before he took the drinks in. But when he went in, they were just sitting and talking.

'I was just saying that I won't be here tomorrow,' Dad said. 'Well, not until the evening. I have to go to the shop. Sue phoned to say she can't come in to work.'

But later Greg remembered the sound of the phone upstairs. 'Nobody rang earlier,' he thought. 'Dad was making a call, not answering one.'

'Dad was making a call, not answering one.'

On Saturday morning Valerie said, 'You're cooking us a nice dinner tonight, Greg, so I'll make lunch today.'

Greg watched her for a minute while she sat at the kitchen

13

Greg watched Val as she sat at the kitchen table.

table, cutting up apples. It was a comfortable, friendly picture, he thought. Then he ran upstairs to his father's bedroom, closed the door and phoned the optician's.

'Can I speak to Mr Barber, please?' he asked.

'I'm afraid he's not in today,' the girl answered. 'Can I help you?'

'No, it's nothing important, thank you,' Greg said.

But it *was* important. It was.

* * *

On Sunday evening Valerie said, 'See you next week.' She was talking to Greg, but it was Dad who answered.

'I'm not sure. Can I phone you?'

'Yes, of course.' Valerie was a little surprised. Greg was

14

very surprised – and at the same time, not surprised at all.

'What's happening next week, then?' he said after Valerie left. 'Where will we be?'

'Here . . . I don't know.' Dad wasn't looking at him. 'Well, perhaps I won't be here next weekend.'

'But I want to see Valerie next weekend.'

'Why don't you go there, then? I'll ask her, if you like. Perhaps she's bored with coming here every week.'

'No, she isn't.'

'Look,' Dad said, 'Valerie's done a lot for us, she's a good friend, but, well, she's only a friend.'

'*Only* a friend? But I thought you – and her . . .'

'No.'

* * *

Later Greg told his friend, Toby, about it.

'Well, your Dad's free now,' Toby said. 'He's come alive again after your Mum's death, and he wants to start again. And Valerie's too old for him.'

'They're the same age. I asked her.'

'Yes, but she looks older than him. I've seen her. He doesn't want people to see him with someone like that. He

'Oh, you are clever,' she said. 'I can't cook anything.'

can get someone better.'

The someone that Dad got was twenty-four and she looked eighteen.

'Oh, you are clever,' she said to Greg when he cooked the dinner that Friday evening. 'I can't cook anything.'

'Why don't you learn?' Greg said coldly. 'I won't always be here.' And neither will you, he said silently to himself.

INVITATION TO TEA

Rockingham Crescent was a street of tall houses on the top of our hill. We lived down the hill and couldn't see the Crescent from our street. It was a place which people talked about but which we never visited. But when my parents gave me my first bicycle and I rode to the top of the hill, I saw that the Crescent was really there. The old houses stood high on the hill and there were plants and flowers everywhere, round every door and window, on every wall from the tops of the houses to the ground. It was like a river of different greens, with here and there bright reds and pinks and yellows. I thought that it was one of the most wonderful places in the world. For a long time I just stood there and looked at it in the warm afternoon sunshine. There was nobody around and the only sounds were birds singing. 'It's like the Gardens of Babylon,' I thought. 'I must come up here again.' It was only five minutes up the hill, but I didn't go back again for three years.

* * *

Patricia Coleman and I began our senior school at the same time, but we were in different classes, so I didn't really get to know her. But in our third year we were in the same French class. We began to talk sometimes and then to walk home

There were plants and flowers everywhere.

together. Pat always turned into another street, but one evening, when we got to the corner, Pat said, 'Have you got to be home early or would you like to come home with me?'

'Well, I've got to be early tonight,' I replied. I looked at the street which she usually turned into. The houses were the same as the houses in my street. My mother always wanted to know things like that.

'Well, come tomorrow, then, for tea,' she said. In those days, when a schoolfriend invited you home to tea, it was a meal at a table, with bread and butter.

When I told my mother, she wanted to know Pat's address and what her father's job was. Pat never talked about her father, so I didn't know what he did. I knew he wasn't dead, so I thought, 'Perhaps he's in prison!'

My mother took some time to decide, but, in the end, she said that I could go to Pat's. I had to be home by half-past six. So, on Friday night I went home with Pat. While we walked through the streets, we were busy doing our French homework together. But, suddenly, I looked up from my book and for the first time, I saw that we were at the top of the hill. Just then Pat said, 'We live round the corner, in Rockingham Crescent.'

I was afraid to look at the Crescent again after all this time, but everything was the same. Perhaps the houses were a little smaller than I remembered them, but I was older and bigger now. The green and red leaves of the plants were

We were busy doing our French homework together.

everywhere, hiding the windows, but everything looked beautiful in the soft autumn sun.

Pat's house was the second one along the Crescent. But when we got to the front door, I saw that the front garden was full of old bicycle wheels and bottles and old boxes. And there was a broken window, grey with dirt. In the front

21

garden next door I could see an old bed. I was very surprised. What would the inside of the house be like? I asked myself.

The hall was dark and narrow. There was no carpet and there were old bicycles everywhere, some without wheels. Through an open door I could see a room, but it was empty and it had no floor. We went upstairs and I followed Pat into another room. It had a floor and a window and walls, and it was crowded with chairs, a table, a big bed, cupboards, clothes – everything you could think of. It was October and

This one room was Pat's home!

it was warm, but Pat began to light the fire. The wood looked like pieces from the floor of the room downstairs.

'Would you like some tea?' she asked. I thanked her and she went to get some water. While she was out of the room, I looked quickly round. There was a cupboard with some cups and plates in it, and a little food. There was another, bigger cupboard with a small bed in it, and through the window I could see down into the wild back garden. There was a little wooden house there – the toilet.

I began to understand. This one room was Pat's home!

Pat came back and put the saucepan on the little fire. It took a long time for the water to get hot. When the tea was ready, Pat brought out a plate with four biscuits on it. We ate one each very carefully.

Conversation was difficult.

Pat brought out a plate with four biscuits on it.

'Have you lived here long?' I asked.

'About two years,' Pat replied. 'We're moving soon,' she went on quickly. 'Mummy doesn't really like it up here. We came here because of Daddy's work, you know.'

She watched my face, but I was learning, and didn't say anything.

I was thinking about my mother, and all her questions when I got home: What was the house like? What did you have for tea? What does her father do? I couldn't tell my mother any of this.

It was beginning to get dark and it was difficult to see in the room. 'Shall I put the light on?' I asked. But at once I knew it was a stupid question, because, of course, there *were* no lights.

'Oh, no,' she said quickly. 'It's nice like this.'

It was very quiet in the Crescent – silent. In my street there was always some noise – voices, shouts, radios, cars.

'Mummy will be back soon,' said Pat. 'I'll just wash these cups and things.'

Where was Mummy? 'Shall I help?' I said.

'No thank you,' she replied quickly. She went out of the room and down the stairs, and then I understood. There was no water in the house. She had to get it from the street.

Pat came back with the cups. 'What time did you say you had to be home?' she asked.

'Half-past six,' I answered.

'It's getting near that now, isn't it?' she said. We both knew that it was only twenty to six, but I was ready to go.

'Yes. Time for me to go,' I said, and I looked round for my schoolbag. But just then we heard a door close. Someone was coming upstairs. I looked up and saw that Pat was really unhappy. She gave me my bag, and I could see that she wanted me to leave quickly. But it was too late. The door opened and a woman came in. Behind her there was a little boy of about five. The boy was tired, the woman looked only half alive. She stood there in her old cheap clothes, her face grey and empty. The face of a person who could no longer fight, or laugh, or hope. She was about thirty-five, but she looked like an old, old woman.

She looked at me for a minute or two and then she spoke. 'Why, Patsy, is this a schoolfriend?' She held out a very thin hand to me. 'How do you do?' she said.

She spoke nicely, like Pat.

'How do you do?' I replied, shaking the thin hand. 'I'm sorry I've got to go. My mother . . .'

'Yes. It's getting dark,' she answered.

'I'll see you on Monday, then,' Pat said.

When I went out, I heard Mrs Coleman cry, 'Oh, Patsy! How could you?'

'She's my friend,' Pat said quietly.

'But to bring someone to this place – and you lit the fire! Those were the last pieces of wood!'

26

The boy was tired, the woman looked only half alive.

I wanted to get away as quickly as I could, but when I was out of the house I walked along the Crescent. And I could see now that no one lived there. All the houses were dirty, dead, and empty. From down the hill I looked back up, and

I could see now that no one lived there.

28

suddenly the Crescent looked like the Gardens of Babylon again, as beautiful as on that warm summer's afternoon three years ago.

* * *

'You're early,' my mother said.

'Yes. I've got a lot of homework,' I replied.

'Did you have a nice time?'

'Oh, yes. Wonderful!'

'Is it a nice house?'

'Lovely. At the top of the hill. I came back along Rockingham Crescent. Does no one live there now?'

'No. Not for about two years. It's a terrible place. They'll pull it all down one of these days. But they were lovely houses once.'

I never went there again and Pat and I were not very friendly after that. I tried to be friendly still, but Pat wasn't really interested.

'They moved,' I said, when my mother asked me why I didn't go again.

But it was some years before I really understood why Pat Coleman asked me to her home that day. She wanted to be like other people just for once, so she asked a friend home for tea.

PARTY WALL

There will be four of them. Daniel decides this immediately; two girls, two men. Last year there were three men. They were very quiet and worked hard at their books. He didn't see them very often because of the high wall between the gardens behind the houses.

Daniel's garden is very small but it's full of flowers. The garden of the next house isn't like that and the first words that Daniel hears this September afternoon are, 'What a terrible place!' It's a girl's voice, high and sweet.

Daniel's garden is very small but it's full of flowers.

'Oh, it's all right, Jenny,' a man replies.

Now the detective work begins; it is important to listen carefully. Daniel sits in his small back room by the open window, and through the open windows of next door he can hear the voices easily. He begins to know them.

'Which room do you want?' someone asks. A third voice. A second girl.

'It doesn't matter, but I want some sun.' That's Jenny again.

'Then you take this one at the back.'

'Next to me,' Daniel thinks. He touches the party wall. On the other side of it is the back bedroom of the house next door.

The window opens beside him. She's getting the sun already. Immediately he looks out of his window, but sees only her slim brown hand on the window-sill.

Daniel sees only her slim brown hand on the window-sill.

'Duncan, are you having the upstairs front room or the downstairs front room?'

'Downstairs. Nearer the bathroom.'

The window of Daniel's small back room is only about a metre away from the window of the next house. When he and his family first moved into the house, Daniel thought that he could make friends with someone through these windows. But there were always students in the other house, not families with children like himself.

He doesn't know the name of the second girl and there's

no one in the fourth bedroom yet, so perhaps there'll be another student later.

'Anna!' Duncan calls. So the second girl is Anna.

* * *

Because the house is on the corner, the front door opens onto a different street from Daniel's, and he can't see people when they come in or go out of the house. But the next morning he hears Jenny call from somewhere inside.

'What time's Russell going to get here?'

'His plane arrives at nine,' Anna answers.

So Russell will be the fourth student.

* * *

The quick way to school does not go past the house next door, but Daniel prefers to go the long way. He wants to walk past their front door. He comes back that way too. No one goes in; no one comes out. But Jenny's window is open.

Daniel goes upstairs. The house is silent. His mother won't be home from work until six o'clock and his father until eight. He lies down on the bed and listens. Perhaps Jenny is lying beside him on her bed. There is only one possible place for the bed in these small rooms, so her bed will be by the wall, like his.

A door closes noisily. Someone has come in. A voice calls, a man, not Duncan. 'Anyone here?' But no one answers him. Russell has come home to an empty house. Ten minutes later he goes out again.

The house is still empty when Daniel goes out to do some running, but when he comes back two hours later there are lights on. Duncan and Russell are in their rooms, and from the garden he can hear Anna's voice in the kitchen. She's looking for a bottle-opener and can't find one. Then Jenny calls, 'I'll go next door and borrow one.'

* * *

Daniel is just going to run to his kitchen to find a bottle-opener for her when he hears Duncan's voice, now in the kitchen too.

'I've found one. In this cupboard.'

Daniel goes up to his room, sits by the open window, and listens while they eat their supper in the garden.

* * *

When the weather gets cold and the windows are closed, Daniel no longer feels that Anna and Russell and Duncan are near. But Jenny feels near, very near in the bed next to him. He can hear her when she moves around her room. She plays her music and sings along with it – not very well. One day, from the bottom of the street, Daniel sees a man in the yellow streetlight, outside the house. Russell? Duncan? He's doing something to his bicycle, but he rides away round the corner before Daniel can get there.

In early December there are a few warm days and the windows are open again. The others get angry with Jenny and shout at her because of the big electricity bill.

Daniel sees a man in the yellow streetlight, outside the house.

'It's all that hot water for your baths – every night!'

So it's Jenny's bath every night, when Daniel hears the water running.

Duncan is the first to go away for the holidays. On Saturday Daniel sees a green car outside and that evening Duncan's window is dark and Daniel doesn't hear his voice. But Christmas is coming, and Anna and Jenny sing in the kitchen. Russell begins to sing too and soon Anna and Jenny stop to listen to him.

'Oh, Russell,' Jenny cries. 'What a wonderful voice you've got! Sing for us again.'

And Russell sings again. He must be a big man because he has a very strong, deep voice.

The next day Anna goes too. It's the last day of school for Daniel. In a week's time it will be Christmas. Daniel's father doesn't understand why he leaves his bedroom window open in cold weather, and his mother asks why he takes the longest way to school. Daniel doesn't explain, and upstairs he opens the window that his father has closed, leans out and listens to the voices in the kitchen.

'Shall we go out tonight?' Russell asks Jenny, but Jenny wants to get ready to leave the next morning.

Russell leaves the day before Christmas Eve and that night every window is dark.

* * *

It is deep winter when they come back. Daniel's window is only open a little at the top. Soon after midnight he wakes. He's sure that he hears a door close and there's a light outside his window. Then he hears someone get into bed. It's Jenny. She's back!

When Daniel comes home from school the next day, he sees a light in Anna's window and in Duncan's too. He goes into the kitchen, gets a cup of coffee and sits down to do his homework. In the next house he can hear a radio. It's playing quietly, and they're getting the evening meal ready. The front door opens and closes. Russell's home again.

One day Daniel nearly sees Jenny. She forgets her key and can't get in. It's raining and she's getting wet. 'Duncan,' she calls, knocking loudly on his window. But it's Russell who

36

One day Daniel nearly sees Jenny.

hears her. Daniel hurries to get to the front window, and just sees her back going round the corner.

A few weeks later a letter comes through the door. Daniel brings it in and his mother opens it. 'They're having a birthday party next door on Saturday,' she says. 'They want to say sorry about the noise.'

'Whose party?' cries Daniel.

'Does it matter?' His mother looks at the letter again. 'Anna Sampson.'

Of course it matters. Daniel wants to know everything. Will they dance? Will Russell sing? Will the party go on all night?

Daniel wakes at three o'clock in the morning and a man's voice speaks in his ear.

'Jenny, please. Why not?'

He doesn't hear the answer, but a door closes and

A man's voice speaks in Daniel's ear.

38

someone goes away. Jenny closes the window noisily.

* * *

When the Easter holiday comes, Duncan is the first to leave. The next day Jenny goes. Then Russell. Does he leave because Jenny's gone?

Anna stays. Poor lonely Anna, Daniel thinks. But she isn't alone. One day he sees a very good-looking young man come out of the house. Daniel stops feeling sorry for Anna.

One morning the green car is back at the door. Duncan has arrived. The young man has gone.

Jenny is the next to come back. Then Russell.

* * *

In May the weather is hot. One evening Jenny comes up to her room early. Daniel leans out a little and sees her arm lying along the open window-sill. She's smoking. Daniel didn't know that Jenny smoked.

Then he hears the others in the kitchen. 'What's the matter with Russell?' Duncan says, and Anna laughs. Daniel goes along to his parents' room and looks across to Russell's window. It's dark, but Russell is in there, alone with his music.

On Friday Daniel is walking past the house and hears Russell in the garden. He's standing below Jenny's window and calling to her softly.

Later Daniel hears voices in Jenny's room.

'I thought you knew,' Russell says.

39

'I don't know what I don't want to know,' Jenny replies. There's a long silence.

'We haven't got much longer,' Russell says.

'Go away,' says Jenny. 'I want to work.'

* * *

When will they all leave this year? July comes and one day Anna goes away in a red car with the young man who came to stay at Easter.

On Saturday morning Daniel hears Jenny shout at someone in her room. 'But you said Wednesday!'

'Well, I got the date wrong,' says Duncan. *Duncan?*

'But you must stay until I leave on Tuesday. You must! I don't want to be alone here with him.'

'Then go out for the evening,' says Duncan. 'And you surely don't think he's going to break your door down in the night, do you?'

Duncan leaves on Monday. His windows are closed. Jenny's window is open but there's no sound from inside the room. All evening Daniel hears the sound of very slow music from Russell's room. Jenny's light comes on at midnight.

The next day a taxi comes and takes Jenny away for ever. It's very quiet in Jenny's bedroom.

But later that evening, very late, Daniel hears a window open beside him. There's an arm along the window-sill of Jenny's room, but it's a man's arm.

There's an arm along the window-sill of Jenny's room,
but it's a man's arm.

'Oh Jenny,' Russell says. 'Oh Jenny, Jenny,' and Daniel
lies and listens to Russell crying himself to sleep on his first
and only night in Jenny's bed.

GLOSSARY

Babylon (the Gardens of)   a place in Persia (now Iraq) more
than 2,000 years ago, with very famous, beautiful gardens
band   a group of people who play music together
electricity   power that comes through wires and can make heat,
light, etc.
fashionable   modern and popular
invite   to ask someone to your house for a meal, a party, etc.
lean   to move the top half of your body forward
next door   the house next to your house
optician   a kind of doctor for the eyes who decides if you need
glasses
party wall   a wall between two homes in the same building
practice   doing something again and again to get it right
rock and roll   popular dance music which began in the 1950s
senior school   a school for older boys and girls (about 11 to 16)
slim   thin, in a nice way

Too Old to Rock and Roll
and Other Stories

ACTIVITIES

Before Reading

1 **Read the story introduction on the first page of the book, and the back cover. How much do you know now about the stories? Match the people with the information.**

Greg / the girl / Daniel

1 _____ goes to a friend's place for tea.

2 _____ listens to people through a wall.

3 _____'s mother died in an accident.

4 _____ likes music and cooking.

5 _____ is interested in the lives of four students.

6 _____ is worried about his father.

7 _____ can hear the people next door, but can't see them.

8 _____ keeps a secret from her mother.

9 _____ thinks Valerie is a nice, kind person.

2 **What is going to happen in these stories? Can you guess? Circle Y (Yes) or N (No) for each answer.**

1 Greg's Dad . . .

   a) joins a rock band. Y/N

   b) falls in love with Valerie and marries her. Y/N

   c) finds a young girlfriend. Y/N

   d) never takes an interest in anything. Y/N

2 The schoolfriend . . .
   a) lives with her boyfriend, not her parents. Y/N
   b) lives with her family in one dirty room. Y/N
   c) has a mother who is in prison. Y/N
   d) tells her friend a terrible secret. Y/N

3 One of the students in the house next door to Daniel . . .
   a) is a thief. Y/N
   b) is unlucky in love. Y/N
   c) has a fight with another student. Y/N
   d) kills another student. Y/N

3 **Who do teenagers talk to about their problems, and who do they tell their secrets to? What do *you* think? Put this list in order under the two headings.**

SECRETS	PROBLEMS

1 A younger brother or sister
2 An older brother or sister
3 Their mother
4 Their father
5 Another person in their family
6 A boyfriend or girlfriend
7 A friend
8 A teacher

While Reading

Read *Too Old to Rock and Roll*. Who said these words in the story, and to whom? Who or what were they talking about?

1 'We need someone here to stop us.'
2 'Can't you keep alive something she loved?'
3 'Well, we've got to be hard with him.'
4 'It's too late to get a tree now.'
5 'I'm sure they'll be happy if I fall under a bus.'
6 'You won't like the music, or the dancing.'
7 '. . . She's a good friend, but, well, she's only a friend.'
8 'Yes, but she looks older than him. I've seen her.'
9 'Oh, you are clever. I can't cook anything.'
10 'I won't always be here.'

Read *Invitation to Tea*. Here are some untrue sentences about the story. Change them into true sentences.

1 When the story-teller first saw Rockingham Crescent, she thought it was a terrible place.
2 The front garden of Pat's house was full of flowers.
3 Pat's family lived in three rooms.
4 Pat lit a fire with some wood from a tree.
5 The two girls sat in the dark because they liked it.

6 The story-teller found it easy to make conversation.

7 After tea, Pat wanted the story-teller to stay.

8 Pat's mother wore expensive clothes and looked young.

9 The story-teller told her mother about Pat's home.

10 After the visit Pat and the story-teller were still friendly.

11 Pat asked the story-teller home for tea because she wanted to be different from other people.

Read *Party Wall*. Then complete the sentences with the names of the correct characters.

Anna / Duncan / Jenny / Russell

1 _____ sleeps in the room next to Daniel's.

2 _____ has a wonderful singing voice.

3 _____ uses a lot of hot water and the others shout at her.

4 _____ asks _____ to go out with him before Christmas.

5 _____ forgets her key one day and knocks on _____'s window, but it's _____ who hears her and lets her in.

6 _____ has a birthday party one Saturday night.

7 _____ sends _____ away from her room at three o'clock in the morning after the party.

8 _____ has a good-looking boyfriend to stay at Easter.

9 _____ calls up to _____'s window in the spring.

10 _____ doesn't want to be alone in the house with _____, and shouts at _____ because he is leaving before her.

11 _____ cries in _____'s room after she leaves.

After Reading

1 In *Too Old to Rock and Roll*, Greg's father spoke to his new girlfriend on the phone (see page 12). Put their conversation in the correct order and write in the speakers' names. Greg's father speaks first (number 6).

1 _____ 'Sure, I'd love to. Shall we meet at the optician's?'

2 _____ 'Yes, I have. I thought we could go for a drive, find somewhere nice to eat . . . Oh, just a minute—'

3 _____ 'Well, would you like to meet me for lunch?'

4 _____ 'Fantastic! I really enjoyed it. Look, I wanted to ask you, Penny – are you free tomorrow?'

5 _____ 'OK. See you then. Bye.'

6 _____ 'Hello, Penny, it's Stephen Barber – Steve. We met at Yvonne's party, you remember?'

7 _____ 'Tomorrow? Yes, I think so.'

8 _____ 'Yes, it was. Sorry, Penny, I've got to go. We've got a visitor. See you tomorrow, about eleven, OK?'

9 _____ 'Great. You've got my address, haven't you?'

10 _____ 'Hi, Steve. Of course I remember. It was a good party, wasn't it?'

11 _____ 'Was that your front door bell, Steve?'

12 _____ 'No, I'm not working tomorrow, so I can come to your house if you like.'

2 In the story *Invitation to Tea*, what was Pat thinking and feeling? Here is a page from her diary. Use these words to complete it (one word for each gap.)

all, always, anything, call, could, father, fire, from, happened, her, homework, invited, life, like, mistake, nice, no, now, outside, want, water, while

Well, I did it. I _____ a schoolfriend home for tea – if you can _____ this place 'home'. Linda and I often do our French _____ together, and I thought we _____ be friends – *real* friends – but I don't think that _____.

She saw everything. She knows that we have _____ lights, no _____ in the house, and that our toilet is _____. She knows that we have to make a _____ with pieces of broken wood _____ the floor.

But she didn't say _____. I waited _____ she drank her tea. I wanted _____ to say, 'Oh, Pat, what's _____? Why do you have to live _____ this?' I wanted to tell her _____ about it.

She didn't _____ to know. She just wanted to leave and go back to her _____, tidy home, with a mother and a _____, and a television and a bicycle . . .

I'm not going to make that _____ again. I know I'll _____ be different from other girls. But why does _____ have to be like this? Why?

3 **Daniel didn't hear everything through the party wall. Here are three short conversations. Complete them with as many words as you like.**

February, in Jenny's room after the party

RUSSELL: Jenny, please. Why not?

JENNY: _____

RUSSELL: I know it's three o'clock in the morning, but . . .

JENNY: _____

RUSSELL: OK, OK, I'm going.

May, in the kitchen

DUNCAN: What's the matter with Russell?

ANNA: _____

DUNCAN: In love? Who with?

ANNA: _____

DUNCAN: No, I didn't. And how does she feel about him?

ANNA: _____

July, in the kitchen

ANNA: Why are you so unkind to Russell?

JENNY: _____

ANNA: Well, tell him that you don't love him.

JENNY: _____

ANNA: And what did he say?

JENNY: _____

ANNA: Breaking his heart? Poor old Russell!

4 Perhaps this is what some of the characters in the stories were thinking. Which six characters are they, and what is happening in the story at this moment?

1 'Oh no, she's brought someone home! How could she do that? I didn't want anyone to know we lived like this. And the wood – she's used the last pieces!'

2 'The poor boy's just sitting there, watching me. He looks so worried. Perhaps he knows that his father never goes to work in jeans. But I won't say anything – I'll just get him a nice lunch . . .'

3 'She thinks I've got a wonderful voice! She's beginning to like me, I'm sure of it. Tomorrow it'll be just her and me in the house. Perhaps she'll come out with me . . .'

4 'It's a lovely house, but I don't think his son likes me very much. He's giving me really angry looks! It's lucky he can cook, because I can't, but I hope he gets more friendly soon . . .'

5 'What's that? There's someone calling my name in the garden . . . Oh no, it's him again! Why can't he leave me alone? I've got to tell him I'm just not interested . . .'

6 'She's back early. It's only six o'clock. She says she had a nice time, but why did she leave early? I'll try and find out more later, when she's done her homework . . .'

5 **Complete this word puzzle with words from the stories. (All the words go down.)**

1 A group of people who play music together. (4)

2 The 'job' of Jenny, Russell, Anna and Duncan. (7)

3 To get hot water, Pat puts this on the fire. (8)

4 Modern and popular. (11)

5 Power that comes through wires to make heat and light. (11)

6 Blue trousers, popular with young people. (5)

7 Green things that grow in the ground. (6)

8 Something to eat with a cup of tea or coffee. (7)

9 Greg's band plays this kind of music. (4)

10 To ask someone to come to your home. (6)

11 The piece of wood at the bottom of a window. (10)

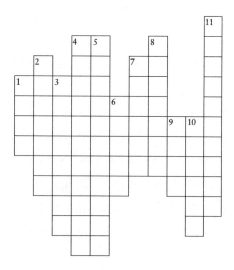

6 Look again at your completed crossword. Can you find the hidden word going across? Here are three clues for this word. Choose and tick the best one.

1 Something that you give to a friend on their birthday.
2 A special food that people eat at Christmas.
3 Beautiful things that go on a Christmas tree.

7 Here are some new titles for the three stories. Which titles go with which stories? Some can go with more than one story. Which are they?

On the Other Side   Love Makes Trouble
Life after Death   Like Other People
A Difficult Visit   The Arm on the Window-Sill
The Schoolfriend   Worrying About Dad
The Girlfriend   Other People's Secrets
Listening to Life   Home

8 Do you agree or disagree with these sentences? Explain why.

1 Greg's Dad was a bad father but Greg was a kind and helpful son.
2 Pat's schoolfriend was right not to ask questions, because saying the wrong thing can hurt people.
3 Daniel was wrong to listen to other people's secrets through the party wall.

ABOUT THE AUTHOR

Jan (Janet Marjorie) Mark was born in 1943 in Hertfordshire, England. She studied art and design, and was an art teacher for several years before she became a writer. She now lives in Oxford, and often visits schools, libraries, and colleges to talk about writing and to give workshops. She is very interested in the teaching of English and does a lot of work with students and teachers on the uses of fiction in the classroom.

Jan Mark's first book was *Thunder and Lightnings* (1976), which won the Carnegie Medal (an important prize for the best children's book of the year). Other titles include *The Ennead* (1978), *The Dead Letter Box* (1982), *Trouble Half-Way* (1985), *Finders, Losers* (1990), and *A Worm's Eye View* (1994). She has written picture books, novels, plays, and television plays, and her books have won several prizes, including a second Carnegie Medal in 1983 for *Handles*. The three stories in this book come from her short-story collection *A Can of Worms* (1990).

Readers of all ages enjoy Jan Mark's stories. She herself has said: 'I write about children, but I don't mind who reads the books.' Many of her stories are about friends – making friends, losing friends, learning to live with friends – and her books are admired for her deep understanding of children and teenagers, and the funny, difficult, and painful things that happen in their lives.

ABOUT BOOKWORMS

OXFORD BOOKWORMS LIBRARY
Classics • True Stories • Fantasy & Horror • Human Interest
Crime & Mystery • Thriller & Adventure

The OXFORD BOOKWORMS LIBRARY offers a wide range of original and adapted stories, both classic and modern, which take learners from elementary to advanced level through six carefully graded language stages:

Stage 1 (400 headwords)	**Stage 4** (1400 headwords)
Stage 2 (700 headwords)	**Stage 5** (1800 headwords)
Stage 3 (1000 headwords)	**Stage 6** (2500 headwords)

More than fifty titles are also available on cassette, and there are many titles at Stages 1 to 4 which are specially recommended for younger learners. In addition to the introductions and activities in each Bookworm, resource material includes photocopiable test worksheets and Teacher's Handbooks, which contain advice on running a class library and using cassettes, and the answers for the activities in the books.

———————————

Several other series are linked to the OXFORD BOOKWORMS LIBRARY. They range from highly illustrated readers for young learners, to playscripts, non-fiction readers, and unsimplified texts for advanced learners.

Oxford Bookworms Starters	*Oxford Bookworms Factfiles*
Oxford Bookworms Playscripts	*Oxford Bookworms Collection*

Details of these series and a full list of all titles in the OXFORD BOOKWORMS LIBRARY can be found in the *Oxford English* catalogues. A selection of titles from the OXFORD BOOKWORMS LIBRARY can be found on the next pages.

The Children of the New Forest

CAPTAIN MARRYAT

Retold by Rowena Akinyemi

England in 1647: King Charles is in prison, and Cromwell's men are fighting the King's men. These are dangerous times for everybody.

The four Beverley children have no parents; their mother is dead and their father died while fighting for the King. Now Cromwell's soldiers have come to burn the house – with the children in it.

The four of them escape into the New Forest – but how will they live? What will they eat? And will Cromwell's soldiers find them?

The Piano

ROSEMARY BORDER

One day, a farmer tells a farm boy to take everything out of an old building and throw it away. 'It's all rubbish,' he says.

In the middle of all the rubbish, the boy finds a beautiful old piano. He has never played before, but now, when his fingers touch the piano, he begins to play. He closes his eyes and the music comes to him – and the music moves his fingers.

When he opens his eyes again, he knows that his life is changed for ever . . .

Matty Doolin

CATHERINE COOKSON

Retold by Diane Mowat

Matty is fifteen and is leaving school in a few weeks' time. He wants to work with animals, and would like to get a job on a farm. But his parents say he's too young to leave home – he must stay in the town and get a job in ship-building, like his father. They also say he can't go on a camping holiday with his friends. And they say he can't keep his dog, Nelson, because Nelson barks all day and eats his father's shoes.

But it is because of Nelson that Matty finds a new life . . .

The Love of a King

PETER DAINTY

All he wanted to do was to marry the woman he loved. But his country said 'No!'

He was Edward VIII, King of Great Britain, King of India, King of Australia, and King of thirty-nine other countries. And he loved the wrong woman.

She was beautiful and she loved him – but she was already married to another man.

It was a love story that shook the world. The King had to choose: to be King, or to have love . . . and leave his country, never to return.